B-24 Bomber Crew

B-24 Bomber Crew

A True Story of the Pacific War with Japan

J. A. Nichols

VANTAGE PRESS
New York

FIRST EDITION

All rights reserved, including the right of
reproduction in whole or in part in any form.

Copyright © 1997 by J. A. Nichols

Published by Vantage Press, Inc.
516 West 34th Street, New York, New York 10001

Manufactured in the United States of America
ISBN: 0-533-12255-4

Library of Congress Catalog Card No.: 96-91045

0 9 8 7 6 5 4 3 2 1

I dedicate this book to my children, Carol, Joan, and Ron. Also to my lovely wife, Marvel, and to my grandchildren who can reflect on our fight during World War II. To Michael and Courtney Johnson, to John, James, and Lindsay Oliver.

I also dedicate this book to my younger sister, Marion, who so tragically passed away.

To those men of the Army Air Force who never came back and also the lucky ones who did.

May they remember that peace was preserved for them by all veterans who fought so valiantly and sacrificed their lives. We should not forget that peace has a price.

Contents

Preface ix
Introduction xi
Author's Note xiii

1. Fly over Nagasaki, Japan 1
2. Joining Air Corps in 1942 4
3. Pre-Flight 7
4. Primary Flight Training 9
5. Select Flight Engineering 11
6. Crew Selection 13
7. Flight Overseas 15
8. First Combat Mission 17
9. Clark Field, Philippines 25
10. Okinawa 56
11. Mission over Shanghai, China 57
12. Weather and Reconnaissance over Tokyo and Nagasaki Bomb Site 63
13. Flight Home 67
14. Separation 69

Appendix: Important Sites 71
Index 77

Preface

This story of World War II in the Pacific area is a true account of events during the Japanese war. This story began over fifty years ago.

I volunteered and served in the Army Air Corps, flying on our B-24 Liberator from Hamilton Air Base, California, to the Pacific theater of war with the Fifth Air Force.

For a young nineteen-year-old, this was a fascinating experience, dangerous flying missions over the vast Pacific, hitting targets in New Guinea, Borneo, Formosa (now Taiwan), China, and Okinawa, Japan.

I kept a diary for each mission. This is why times and dates are precise. Also, I kept the photos of the bombing missions as well as the photos of my military life.

This is not a story of great drama or heroic-type incidents but a story of an average young United States citizen who volunteered at a time when America was at risk of losing its independence to the Japanese and German forces.

Bomber Crew

Pilot:	Leroy Olsak
Co-Pilot:	Charles Alumbaugh
Navigator:	Edward Urbanik
Bombardier:	Ankle Molver
Flight Engineer:	John Nichols
Radio Operator:	Robert Baze

morer: Michael Badolato
Gunner: Robert Arnold
Tail Gunner: Steve Bubicz
Nose Gunner: Francis Smith

B-24 Bomber

Name:	Liberator
Cruise Speed:	Approximately 290 miles per hour
Plane Weight:	55,000 lbs.
Fuel Tanks:	#1 & #4 616 gallons each #2 & #3 556 gallons each Bomb Bay Tanks 391 gallons Wings Tanks 225 gallons each
Total Fuel with 2 Bomb Bay Tanks:	3,576 Gallons
Plane Length:	66'—4"
Plane Height:	17'—11"
Plane Span:	110 feet
Bombs:	Eight (8) 2000-lb. or various types of small bombs
Guns:	Ten (10) 50-caliber machine guns
Range:	Approximately 15 hours flying time 3,000 miles
Altitude:	30,000 feet

Introduction

There were over 18,479 B-24 Liberators built, more military and civilian aircraft than any other plane.

See the picture of the only B-24 still flying today in the world. The B-24 was built by Consolidated Aircraft (now General Dynamics). Such planes were built in San Diego, California; Fort Worth, Texas; Willow Run, Michigan (Ford Motor Company); North American at Fort Worth and Douglas at Tulsa, Oklahoma.

During World War II, B-24's flew more missions and dropped more bombs than any other aircraft.

Decorations

Air Medal (Twice)
Asiatic-Pacific Theater Ribbon with Five Bronze Stars
Philippine Liberation Ribbon with two Bronze Stars

Author's Note

Japan attacked the United States at Pearl Harbor on December 7, 1941. The United States began its war buildup rapidly, the biggest effort the world had ever known.

Meanwhile Europe was involved with its war with Germany and now, the United States was totally involved with both theaters of war, European and Pacific.

In this atmosphere of hasty buildup, I volunteered for the Air Cadet program. Since I was not twenty-one years old, my parents needed to sign their approval. It took a lot of persuasion on my part, but I finally got their signatures and signed up.

B-24 Bomber Crew

1
Fly over Nagasaki, Japan

It was the most unbelievable sight I have ever seen! The B-24 Bomber, of the Fifth Air Force, flying on September 14, 1945 out of Okinawa, was circling over the Nagasaki atom bomb site. Everything was leveled in a perfect circle, reddish in complexion. The only things standing were several factory chimneys. Being round, they withstood the blasts.

The B-24 was a Liberator bomber, a slow-speed (compared to today's) four-engine twin tail, with a crew of ten people: Pilot, Co-Pilot, Radio Man, Navigator, Bombardier, Flight Engineer, Tail Gunner, Turret Gunner, Nose Gunner, and Waist Gunners.

This was a select crew put together for a weather and reconnaissance mission over the Japanese coast. The war was just over, to everyone's relief. The date was August 14, 1945. When we left Matsubi Air Field, Okinawa, earlier that day, we flew northeast toward the east coast of Japan. When we were flying parallel with the coast, a strange sight confronted us. The coast was lined with high cliffs and a number of caves were visible on the cliffs. Outside the caves, men were waving white surrender flags, meaning, don't drop any bombs!

It was a clear day. None of us at that time fully comprehended the great historical event. What mattered to us was that the war was over. We would be going home soon.

Earlier, before the atomic bomb was dropped, we had been stationed at Clark Field, the air base in the Philippines. We were converting the B-24 bomb bays into plywood seats for paratroopers, in preparation for an attack over Japan. We had been practicing this training for at least two weeks. During practice one of the planes crashed near Palawan Islands in the Philippines, killing all troopers and crew.

There is a lot of discussion today regarding the morality of the United States dropping the atomic bombs. There is absolutely no question in my mind about dropping the bombs. It was extremely necessary. I would not be around today if we had not. Just imagine the slaughter resulting from an invasion, slaughter not only of United States personnel but also Japanese. The paratroopers would have been targets as easy as sitting ducks on their way down.

It is easy for people today to say it is immoral, easy for someone not sacrificing his life to say we were wrong. These people were not in harm's way, but for a soldier in combat, it's a different life and feeling. President Truman made the right decision.

The picture of the bomb sites is forever etched on my mind. I would estimate that perhaps 800,000 to 1,000,000 casualties would have resulted for the United States alone if we had invaded Japan, plus over 1,500,000 Japanese. This alone would justify the use of the bombs, whereas only approximately 140,000 people died as a result of the two atomic bomb drops. It is important to remember that the atom bomb saved many lives in the armed services.

Scientists gained an understanding of the basic structure of the atom back during the late 1800s and early 1900s. In 1938 researchers discovered that splitting the nucleus of a uranium atom released a lot of energy.

By early 1939, before the start of World War II, physicists in the United states had become aware of the potential military application of nuclear energy. In order to beat Germany, to develop this, the United States set up the Manhattan Project, to design and build a fission bomb. On July 16, 1945, the United States exploded the first experimental nuclear device in Alamogordo, New Mexico. This was a 22-kiloton implosion-type fission device.

The first nuclear weapon used by the United States against

Japan was a gun-type fission bomb. It had a yield of 13 kilotons. The first bomb was dropped from a B-29 on Hiroshima on August 6, 1945.

Three days later, on August 9, 1945, another B-29 dropped a 22-kiloton implosion-type fission bomb on Nagasaki. These bombs largely destroyed both cities, but the number of deaths differed greatly. The small bomb killed from 70,000 to 100,000 people in Hiroshima, which had a flat terrain. The larger bomb killed about 40,000 in Nagasaki, which had a hilly terrain. Other people in both cities died later of injuries and radiation.

On August 14, 1945 Japan agreed to surrender. The surrender was proper for Japan since many lives were spared. The prolonging of the war would have been senseless. So, what Japan had started by attacking Pearl Harbor ended in their total defeat.

During this special flight on September 14th, we flew over Tokyo. Tokyo Bay was filled with United States Navy ships, aircraft carriers, battleships, cruisers, destroyers, and miscellaneous vessels. We flew at 900 feet over Tokyo. The sights were incredible! Trains and trolleys were operating. We could see the people walking about. No one looked up at our plane. My feelings were that they were humiliated in defeat.

Strangely, though the business districts as well as the factory areas were leveled and burned out, the countryside, however was not damaged. This was due to the United States care that no such civilian areas were to be bombed.

When we returned to base after a long, tiring flight, everyone in the squadron wanted to know our experience, for it was a great and unusual opportunity to be chosen for a this special flight. I felt greatly relieved that finally the fighting was over and we could fly over Japan without worrying about flack and Zeros attacking.

2
Joining Air Corps in 1942

I had lived through the Great Depression of the 1930s as a teenager. My father and his two brothers had a variety store and fruit and vegetable route. While I was going to school, I had to work on Saturdays on my father's truck preparing orders for the customers while other boys my age were playing baseball. On Saturdays I had to wake up at 4:00 A.M. to go to the market with my father to prepare for the route. During the weekdays, after school I had to work in my family's store until 8:00 P.M.

However, because of how hard it was to make a living, I had basic values imbedded into my character. Anybody who did not live through the Depression cannot understand how rough it was. My father and his brothers lost the store and business because people did not pay their bills. They trusted the customers on credit and were left holding the bag. It was a very emotional and sad time when with only $25 in his pocket my father moved the family from Quincy, Massachusetts, to Boston in a change of environment from a single family house to a Boston flat.

In 1942, before I graduated Boston English High School, which is the oldest public high school in the United States, I became very interested in art. The person who influenced my interest in art was Mr. Adams, the art teacher. He seemed genuinely interested in helping me to pursue this career, so much so that he was influential and obtained a scholarship for me to attend the Massachusetts School of Art.

When I graduated from Boston English, I got a job for the

summer for a couple of months before starting art school. However, because of the war, I was driven by a strong urge to join the Army Air Corps. Before I was called to duty, I visited the school and saw Mr. Adams that fall. When I told him about my enlistment, he looked at me sadly, with what I thought were tears in his eyes and said, "John, you are not a fighter, you are an artist."

Today I often think of this encounter and know that he meant, "Why should a young fellow go to war and not pursue his goal?" Mr. Adams was genuinely a man of the arts.

As a result of his influence, I still paint as a hobby in an amateurish way, even though I attended Northeastern University and pursued an engineering profession after the war.

I joined the Army Air Force as an Air Force Cadet, volunteering in 1942 in Boston. I was so anxious to be called in for duty that I was puzzled when my friends who hated to be drafted were called before me. The Air Corps was selective and needed time for classes to begin. I constantly checked to find out why I was not called. Finally I was, on March 6th, 1943.

When I enlisted for the service, I went to North Station for gathering and then traveled by train to Fort Devens in Massachusetts. At Devens we stayed overnight. During the evening we were so cold in our barracks that we tore down the wooden shelves there and used the wood for a fire in the stove. Coal was not available. We still wore our civilian clothes. The next day we boarded a train for Nashville, Tennessee, where after a day and one-half ride, we arrived for processing and were issued uniforms. We began a rapid training program for a few days and then were shipped to Maxwell Air Base in Montgomery, Alabama. In Montgomery we were assigned to our company and started drilling and classes.

At Boston High School, we were trained for military parades and drill. All Boston schools were in this program. I became a captain of a company in high school. Because of this training, I was assigned a company in the cadets.

Nashville was a staging area for the cadets. There we were issued our uniforms, toilet articles, personal gear, and instructions on military life. This was like boot camp, only very simply a sorting point. We spent approximately two weeks in Nashville—we were given our Air Cadet Wings and allowed to visit the city. All cadets were invited to the coming-out balls where the Southern beauties treated the cadets to dances and refreshments. The people were extremely friendly and made the cadets feel wanted in their city.

3
Pre-Flight

It was not long before we were ordered to Maxwell Air Base in Montgomery, Alabama. Maxwell Pre-Flight School was operated like West Point Academy—strict methods of treating upper and lower classmen. New cadets were severely harassed by upper classmen. This trained cadets to see if they could "take it." If there were any instances of cheating or rowdy actions, cadets were "drummed" out of their class for service in other branches of the armed forces.

During a "drubbing out of a cadets," all the squadrons were called out for a parade while the drummed cadet was stripped of his Air Corps wings and buttons on his jacket and sent on his way to another branch of the service.

Everyone was called "Mister." If you wanted leave to go to the city, you had better not cross the upper classmen. The upperclassmen from the South usually lined up lower classmen from the North and asked "Who won the Civil War?" If you did not answer "The South," no pass for town that weekend.

During pre-flight we attended classes in math, navigation, physics, etc., as well as learning the Morse Code. After we completed pre-flight, we were assigned to primary flight school where we flew PT-17 Stearman trainers. The PT-17 was a bi-winged, open-cockpit plane.

I was assigned to the Douglas, Georgia, primary flight school. After learning the mechanics of the PT-17, we began to fly with an instructor. On the first two flights, I became very air sick. So while flying, I put my chin on the edge of the cockpit to empty my stomach; the instructor kept turning sharply to the left to avoid spill on the tail. Looking down on the ground, which was swirling round and round, I became more sick and kept emptying my stomach. After we landed it was customary for the student pilot to pick up a mop and brush and clean the side of the plane. This was very embarrassing.

One day, after eight and one-half hours of flying with the instructor, including practice landings, he motioned to me to taxi towards the side of the runway. He got out and told me to go ahead and fly solo. At this time my knees began shaking as I taxied to take off. At that time I didn't even know how to drive a car since my family was poor and could not afford a family car, let alone fly a plane. As I gave full throttle and lifted the tail off the ground, I could not think of anything but to try to do a good solo flight. I pulled the stick back and started to climb. I turned left and another left to keep in the landing pattern. As I made another left, I started to descend on a landing leg. I cut the throttle back and glided toward the runway. I hit the ground and slightly bounced a couple of times but finally held ground and pulled the stick back to drop the tail. My heart was in my mouth as I taxied towards the instructor. He gave me a thumbs up as he climbed aboard and we taxied to the ramp. After I soloed I was overjoyed as I got off the plane and headed for the briefing room. I couldn't wait to write to my family about this solo.

4
Primary Flight Training

During the next few weeks, I practiced all kinds of maneuvers, pylon 8, chandels, rolls, spins, emergency landings, etc. Then we were told that the Army Air Corps had too many pilots and they might have to give us other choices: Navigator, Bombardier, or Flight Engineer. I chose Flight Engineering and was transferred to Goldsboro Air Corp Base for training. I entered in the instructor training program and took classes in flight engineering.

During our primary flight training, we had various experiences. We used to fly and practice our maneuvers in assigned areas of the field. One particular thing we used to do was fly over the cotton-growing fields. While the workers would pick cotton, we "buzzed" them for fun. We would dive at the workers and fly over their heads while they hit the ground. Looking back we could see cotton flying all over. It was fun for us, but we scared the hell out of the workers. One cadet was washed out because he spotted a car on the highway and he dived toward it. When he caught up with it, he hopped over and landed in front of the car, then took off. It so happened that the commandant of the school was in the car and he spotted the plane's number. As all planes had assigned numbers, this cadet was washed out.

When I started to fly with the instructor, maybe on the second trip, he talked to me over the ear phones, which were actually flex tubing to our ears. He said, "Make sure your belt is tight." As I nodded and began to tighten the belt, he snap-rolled the plane. My belt was loose and I gulped as I struggled to hang on. My loose articles in my jacket fell off as I held my breath. I always tightened my belt from then on.

One other cadet was washed out, this time because during his solo flight, the poor guy had a perception problem. He thought the ground was near, when he was actually twenty-five feet from the ground. He would come down, nearly hit the ground, and turn 90 degrees off and fly over towards the tower. The red flag would go up and all planes knew to stay away from the air field until he finally landed.

Another cadet was washed out because he got air sick all the time. Actually only 25 percent of the cadets made it to the next step. Then of course, there were too many pilots, so most were transferred to navigation, bombardiering, or flight engineering.

Because of my "mechanical flying" and too many pilots in the program, I was out of the pilot program and offered navigation, bombardiering, or flight engineering. Thinking that engineering would be useful after the war, I selected it.

I was stationed for a brief period of six weeks in Fort Myers, Florida. There we trained for advanced gunnery on a B-17 and a B-24 bomber.

Our training consisted of targets in the Gulf of Mexico. These were tow targets and stationery targets on the water. I enjoyed this duty since the weather was perfect and the duty was not severe. Even though the B-24 carried more bombs and was slower, the B-17 was sturdy and as mentioned by others could fly with holes in the wings.

5
Select Flight Engineering

After the primary flight training in Douglas, Georgia, I was sent to Seymore Johnson Field in Goldsboro, North Carolina, as an instructor on aircraft. One day while in the a waist of the plane, one student picked up what he thought was a speaking tube on the side wall and began to speak "gunner to pilot, gunner to—" he did not finish. He had put on his face a funnel used for urinating while in flight. As soon as he smelled the awful odor, he dropped the funnel, but not before he left a black ring around his mouth. Planes had this type of gadgets for emergency urination while flying. The student never forgot this and he was very embarrassed.

Soon afterwards, I was ordered to go to California for assignment to gunnery school and eventually to Douglas Air Craft A-20 factory in Santa Monica, California. After four weeks at Douglas, they shipped me to Mather Air Corp base near Sacramento, California. There we were assigned to a B-24 bomber crew for shipment to the Pacific theater of war. Typical armed forces: train for an A-20 aircraft and land on a B-24 squadron.

While at the Douglas Aircraft factory in Santa Monica, California, the Air Corps had me studying the A-20, an attack bomber, twin-engine aircraft. I spent four weeks in the factory getting familiar with the plane. It was strange to see the production line with girls in fur jackets working on a small area of the plane. This was my best duty. We were treated royally by the citizens of Santa Monica. During leaves, all we had to do was stand on the sidewalk at the gate and people would pick us up for a ride to town or their homes. We did not have to thumb our way around.

The Santa Monica area was a very pleasant place to live. Warm during the day and cool at night for sleeping. I fell in love with the area and swore I would return. My buddy and I looked at a lot in San Fernando Valley. They wanted $2000. What a bargain! Today it would be half a million or more.

I was sent to Riverside Air Base, Riverside, California. We used this base for practice flights and practice bombing missions to Washington State, Arizona, Palm Springs. etc. One day while we were resting in our barracks, we heard this weird noise. A plane was in trouble. We ran outside just in time to see a B-25 bomber crash between two barracks. It left a hole about twenty feet deep as it blew up. The two barracks were damaged. This is the closest I came to being killed, staying on my bunk. It was sickening to see dead people with their bodies charred and smelling like a barbecue. Later on I found out a friend of mine from Connecticut was killed in the plane crash.

During training at Riverside Air Base, California, besides practicing bombing runs to various cities like Seattle, Washington, Phoenix, Arizona; Portland, Oregon; Boise, Idaho, etc., we were scheduled to fly to Palm Springs, California, to deliver spare parts for a B:24 that had been forced to land there in an emergency landing. At that time there was nothing around the air strip. Today it has been built up so much that you could not recognize the area. We flew low between mountains where air currents were very strong and the plane bounced around. In order to land at Palm Springs, we had to approach low between mountains.

6
Crew Selection

When our crew was assembled, we shipped out to Hamilton Air Base near San Francisco for flying overseas. On February 5, 1945, we were assigned plane No. 44-5038, a B-24M. While waiting to fly our plane overseas in Hamilton Air Base in San Francisco, we had leaves. One time we visited a hotel where the USO was giving a party for servicemen. The place was not too big but crowded with GIs. There were four of us on leave and looking for a party. So we stopped and each one bought a bottle of liquor. When we stumbled into this gathering Mac, the nose gunner, suggested we dump all of the four bottles in the fruit punch bowl on the table, which we did unnoticed. After a couple of hours, everyone was high, including the USO girls.

On February 15, 1945, we flew for a fuel-consumption mission and landed at Mather Field, Sacramento. On February 28, 1945, at 00:30, we took off and flew for approximately three hours. We ran into a violent storm and were forced to return to Hamilton Air Base. When we were scheduled to take off again at 22:30, we had a taxi accident. The right wing tip hit a flag pole and was damaged, cancelling the trip until it was repaired.

During the first attempted flight, we also ran into a problem. One hour after take off, the nose wheel indicator light showed it was not locked on the retracted position. I went down to the nose wheel well and the mechanism had jammed. After a few attempts, I finally succeeded to have it lock. I took my gloves off, and when I touched the cold metal, my right hand skin came off. At that altitude the metal parts were frozen.

7
Flight Overseas

On March 4, 1945, took off at 02:25 for Honolulu. On the way over, Navy ships were located every five hundred miles for signals and rescue missions. Two of our twelve planes went down. When flight engineers transferred fuel from wing tanks to main tanks, they accidentally shut off main fuel lines and we could see and hear on our intercoms the alarm those crews showed as they glided down to ditch. It was sad to see our men yelling and screaming as they ditched their bombers. We did not know if they survived or not. Much later, one of the crews joined us in the Philippines; they made it but the second crew never did make it. We landed at Honolulu Naval Air station at 15:15 State time. The trip took 13 hours and 25 minutes. There we spent two days.

On March 7 we took off for Canton Island, a small island southwest of Hawaii. We spent the night there. This island was so small that it barely had room for a runway and I recall seeing only one tree. On March 8 we took off for Tarawa and arrived approximately six hours later.

Tarawa was a terrible sight! During the invasion our Marines were trapped in the water with all their gear. Bodies were still floating on the water. As we were landing, Army bulldozers were pushing dead Japanese soldiers in a large pit. The battle must have been fierce. The Japanese concrete boxes must have been about six feet thick as we saw evidence of Navy shells hitting the walls and only penetrating about three feet. This explained why the Marines had no chance as they came toward the boxes. I can never erase the picture of utter destruction from my mind. War is a terrible thing.

On March 9 we took off for the Admiralty Islands and landed at Los Negros to spend the night. On March 10th we arrived at our destination on a small island off New Guinea called Biak. We spent six days at Biak. The Japanese were still in the hills very close by. We had many laughs at the natives. They were huge and strong. They moved our tent floor which was made of wood to another location for our just giving them three razor blades! They smoked corn-whiskers rolled on a newspaper as cigarettes. They would do anything for a few gadgets such as razor blades or beads and K-rations.

On March 16, we took off from Biak and arrived by flying a C-47 from Biak to Nadzab in New Guinea for special training. We left our B-24 there to pick up on the way up north.

On March 26, we visited a post at Lae, New Guinea. The Red Cross had a nice club for the GIs. They even had ice water, which was very rare in New Guinea. As we traveled on the road, we could see bananas growing on both sides of the road. Then we found out that the Japanese had bombed Biak. We got out just in time.

On March 27, we started school for .50-caliber machine gun training and .45 pistol firing.

On March 31 our radar crew was broken up and the radar operator was taken from us. We were transferred to a regular combat crew and assigned to Section A-7.

8
First Combat Mission

Diary Excerpts

APRIL 1, 1945

Intelligence lectured us on the history of the South Pacific theater. They briefed us on escape and evasion, flack and malaria control, etc.

APRIL 2, 1945

This day I had .45 pistol firing on target range, improving all the time. The .45 was a pistol with a lot of "kick." We were taught to squeeze the trigger for better results.

APRIL 3, 1945

I had practice on a skeet range, shooting shot guns from a moving truck. The back of the truck had a safety rail that you stood by. As the truck traveled in an oblong range, wires tripped skeet so you could shoot at it. You never knew which direction the skeet was coming from; you had to be alert. This practice is to sharpen your ability to lead properly and fire. The skeet houses were hidden, and a spring-loaded clay skeet would be released when the wire tripped the mechanism to let the skeet go in different directions.

APRIL 11, 1945

Our crew flew two orientation missions and made two landings to train for combat and become oriented with the New Guinea area.

During our stay at Nadzab Air Field in New Guinea, between missions, we had survival training in the surrounding jungle. We took overnight trips to train in living off the land. One day we came upon a patch full of small tomatoes, the size of plums. Apparently someone at one time had tomatoes and spread the seeds. It was strange to see so deep into the jungle. We had to be alert for snakes, mosquitoes, and other dangers. The jungle was very dense and we had to use machetes to cut our way through the trails. The heat was unbearable. We slept in open tents with mosquito netting over our bunks while at the base.

Typical Mission

The day before the mission, we met for briefing purposes regarding the target, expected interception, expected flack and weather. We were told the type of bombs to carry, flight time, length of flight, plus secondary targets to hit, etc.

The planes were prepared by the ground crews, loaded with gas and bombs, plus live ammunition for the 50-caliber guns. Usually missions began for take off by six o'clock in the morning.

One of the duties the flight engineer had, was that before we landed he was to go to the rear of the plane so he could look at the landing gear to see if it was down and locked in position. Many times I and the waist gunner, Arnold, had a joke to play on the ball gunner. I would look at the wheels and hold my head in horror, making believe that there was something wrong with the plane. Meantime Arnold would keep a close eye on the ball gunner since he, one time had taken his chest parachute, hooked it on his gear, and opened the rear latch to bail out. He would have bailed out if Arnold had not grabbed his harness and held him inside the plane.

The ball gunner thought there was something wrong with the plane and wanted to bail out.

Flying toward the target was tiresome. The flight engineer had to constantly check performance of engines, fuel consumption, proper working of all systems, such as hydraulic, electrical, etc. It was necessary to check on the bomb load for proper security and safety. The flight engineer constantly helped the pilot, giving assistance to the engine operation, flaps, and landing gear.

Before we approached the target, the crew took their battle position. The bombardier checked his equipment, the navigator checked his bearing, the gunners took their stations. The flight engineer used the upper turret guns, just behind the pilot and co-pilot. The two waist gunners took their station on each side of the aircraft. The tail gunner placed himself in the tail section. The nose gunner was ahead of the bombardier section. The ball gunner injected himself in the open hatch. The ball gunner had the most dangerous position. He was under the belly of the plane and felt as though he was hanging by his thumbs. It was a scary location. I actually had to stuff him in the ball turret by pushing with my feet. All the crew was concerned because we might not be protected from the bottom of the plane. Fortunately we did not have any problems.

Over the target we kept an eye open for any Zero attacks. One time we encountered four Zeros that kept behind us, swaying left and right. We thought at any moment they were going to attack. However, each plane had eight .50-caliber guns (not counting the nose guns) aimed at the Zeros. Six B-24s in formation made it a total of 48 guns aimed and swaying at the Zeros, so you can see why the Zeros did not attack. It would have been suicide.

After the bombs dropped and for approximately one hour, we kept our stations. Then, when it was safe, we returned to our regular duties. Mostly the gunners did not have any function, on the way back, except to be passengers. However, before landing all .50-caliber guns had to be cleared and secured. One time when we landed, after a mission, as we prepared to leave the plane, a .50-caliber gun fired by itself, due to the heat, which discharged a shell accidentally. Fortunately no one was hit.

If flying time was long, the flight engineer closely checked the fuel tanks, calculated the return trip consumption, and transferred fuel from wing tanks to main tanks.

After landing we all met and were debriefed for any intelligence information, then given a small shot of liquor to settle our nerves.

I had to inspect the plane before we took off on a mission. The fuel tanks had to be drained slightly to get rid of the water, which condensed inside the fuel tanks. This was done by a pet cock valve under the wings. Since water would be heavier than gasoline, it settled on the bottom of the plane tanks. If not drained properly, the water could cause an engine failure.

Preparing for a Combat Mission

The stress is unbearable before a mission. When you are young (I was 19 years when I volunteered and 20, and 21, when I was in combat), you tend to be gung-ho and not think of your safety. I often wondered why the older men, say 30 years or older, seemed to be more cautious before missions.

We were briefed the day before as to details of the next mission. We met in the briefing room and were advised on flack possibility, weather, and length of flight, plus primary and secondary targets. We were also briefed on emergency landings, ditching over water, what to expect for rescue, etc.

Our parachute packs were equipped with K-rations, Chinese, Borneo, and New Guinea money, survival kits with fish hooks, shark repellents, machetes, survival books, etc. I don't think the yellow shark repellant really repelled sharks. I think this was a psychological approach only. We also were taught to eat berries and leaves if we parachuted over land.

Usually there were twelve planes in a formation, sometimes less than twelve when planes had problems. The flight engineer, which I was, always inspected the plane one hour before flight, plus checking proper loading of plane for center of gravity. We checked the bomb bays for proper loading and inspected the bomb shackles for proper mounting and safety wires on bombs.

In one of the missions over a target, with the bomb bay doors open, we noticed a bomb hung up on the solenoid shackle. There were two shackles for each bomb. One shackle had let the bomb drop, but the other had hung up. This of course is very dangerous, in case the safety wire had come loose and the air stream moved the bomb sideways.

I quickly picked up a screwdriver and headed for the bomb bay catwalk. Again you see the ground twenty thousand feet below—very dangerous with the bomb bay doors open. I jammed the screwdriver against the solenoid latch and fortunately it let the bomb drop. We sighed with relief. I had to be careful when the bomb fell that I was not snagged and pulled down with it. The nose of the bomb had a safety wire through the safety latch. The wire stayed with the plane as the bomb left the bomb bay, making the bombs armed to explode on contact.

At twenty thousand foot elevation we had to use oxygen. When traveling about the plane, we used to carry on oxygen bottles. This made it very uncomfortable walking, especially on the bomb bay catwalk.

Flight Gear

Flying suit with pockets on side, pant legs, etc.
Back parachute with life survival items in suit, such as machete, Chinese money, fishing hooks, survival book, concentrated candy, bar of chocolate, and signaling mir-

ror with cross hair for aiming at the sun in case you were down and signaling for rescue.

.45-Colt (extra clip of bullets)
Flack helmet
Flack chest
Extra chest parachute (near your station)
Oxygen mask
Goggles
Sunglasses

Diary Excerpts

First Mission

APRIL 15, 1945

Today we began our combat missions. We flew over Wewak, New Guinea where the Japanese still held an airport and base. We took off at 8:00 and hit target at 10:45. We dropped twenty fragmentation bombs over their headquarters. On the way back, we fired over 200 rounds of .50-caliber ammunition at a tow target. Our plane was a B-24J. The moving target would be towed several hundred feet from the tow plane. Wewak is located on the northeastern side of New Guinea. Our base was on the southeastern area of New Guinea.

The weather was perfect: no cloud cover. Being near the equator, the temperature was unbearable. Finally we are getting in the real war. We did not know what to expect, but finally after all our training, we are now in the real bombing missions against the enemy. Will we run into any trouble? Plane malfunction? Or enemy resistance? It was exiting and thrilling to know that now we were hurting the Japanese.

On the first combat mission, you feel kind of uncertain,

butterflies in your stomach. There is danger that almost anything wrong could happen to you and the crew. You only hope that God can protect you.

Second Mission

APRIL 16, 1945

We had a second mission over Rabaul, New Britain Island. We hit the target at approximately 11:00, no opposition whatsoever, although we were warned to expect ack-ack and fighters. We dropped bombs at a point off Rabaul Harbor. You could see the bombs hitting the target. This was a strange feeling to know that you were really hurting the enemy. When the bombs left the plane, the plane would lift up as the load was dropped. Flying twenty thousand feet elevation, the bombs would take some time to hit the ground, so we could see their explosion. It was especially gratifying when direct hits were made. Rebaul is on the eastern side of New Guinea.

Since we did not receive any resistance from the Japanese on the first mission, we were less concerned on the second mission. Again the weather was perfect for flying. Rabaul was a Japanese stronghold that was leap-frogged by MacArthur on his flight northward. Rabaul is where the Japanese Admiral Yamamoto was killed by our P-38 planes when he was on a flight to inspect this area. The U.S. had broken their secret code and had advance notice of Yamamoto's flight.

Third Mission

APRIL 17, 1945

On this day we were lead ship on a flight of twelve planes. We hit Wewak dropping twenty fragmentation bombs. We hit the target at 10:45. No opposition. I said this is really good, no fight from the enemy. It is now routine for us to drop bombs and have no opposition. We feel like now we are veterans. When we arrived for the landing, a plane ahead of us had some problems, so we circled around for almost an hour before we could land. After we landed and debriefed, we had lunch and rested for the next mission.

APRIL 22, 1945
On this day we left Nadzab for Biak. We were assigned to Fifth Air Force V Bomber Command of Twenty-second Group, which is stationed in Clark Field, Philippines. The heat was unbearable as we kept waiting. I was very impatient to get moving.

APRIL 26, 1945
Left Biak and landed at Palau Island on a C-47 Transport plane. Since there were many planes available in Clark Field, Philippines, the crews were transported by passenger planes to Clark Field.

9
Clark Field, Philippines

APRIL 27, 1945

We left Palau and landed at Leyte, the Philippines. We left Leyte and landed at Lengeyan. Then we left Lengeyan and landed at Clark Field, Philippines. Met our squadron and were assigned to the Thirty-third Bomb Squadron, called the Red Raiders. The squadron lived in an open area full of tents. In the center was a mess hall, also showers, field hospital, and various shacks. The briefing buildings were in the field itself, which we traveled by trucks. The logo for the Thirty-third Squadron was the head of a bearded Viking.

4th Mission

MAY 1, 1945

On a special select crew, my fourth mission was over Shanghai, China. We took off at 18:15, ship No.612 carrying four thousand-pound bombs. This plane was heavily loaded, so much so that we could not gain altitude because of two extra bomb bay tanks, for the long mission. At this point we dropped one bomb over the Lengeyan Gulf plus a lot of .50-caliber rounds. We even dropped our ack-ack chest protectors, steel helmets, and other unessential equipment in order to gain altitude. As we did all this and burned more fuel, we began to gain altitude.

Our mission was to fly towards the Yangtze River, find the oil tanks, drop bombs and strafe the oil tanks. This was a single plane flight. We were to fly at fifteen hundred feet, which is low for a B-24 bomber, but Intelligence wanted us to surprise the Japanese, since they never expected a single plane to be that far away from a United States base. We added two (2) bomb bay fuel tanks to reach the destination, which was very far. Everyone on the crew was very concerned about the outcome. Not only about the length of the flight but the chances of being shot down over China.

We arrived at our destination at 1:30 A.M., May 2. We flew up and down the Yangtze River in order to find the targets. However it was so hazy we were unable to find the oil tanks. On our second trip up the river, we noticed a vessel on the river, all lit up. Since we had no choice, we dropped three (3) thousand-pound bombs from an altitude of fifteen hundred feet. Even if the bombs missed, I'm sure the vessel sank because as we dropped our bombs, we banked sharply and dropped to approximately five hundred feet. Before we dropped our bombs on the way down the Yangtze River, we noticed a plane flying near us with his lights on. We also put on our landing lights, making believe we were friendly. This worked.

As we headed towards the open ocean flying at approximately five hundred feet, we were all waiting to be attacked by fighters. However we were now breathing a sigh of relief. This mission lasted over fifteen hours flying time, for those days a very long flight. We were dog tired when we landed. Not too much damage was done, however. Psychologically the Japanese knew we could strike that deep in enemy territory. I am sure it sent fear in their hearts. For a U.S. plane to be dropping bombs that far from an American base was not expected by the Japanese.

MAY 6, 1945

While at Clark Field, our crew visited Angeles and San Fernando, two small towns nearby. The Filipinos were so glad that we liberated them from the Japanese they would do anything for the GI's. Horse-drawn taxis were everywhere. We tried some fried chicken, which tasted good compared to our chow.

We heard a story about one GI in our squadron who was busted from Sergeant to P.F.C. because he coerced a few Filipino girls to work for him for a few cans of Spam. His mistake was that he used an old shack near a railroad station as his headquarters for the girls. When a line appeared approximately 50 feet long of waiting GI's, the squadron commander could not help but notice and he busted the enterprise.

On one side trip we had while at Clark Field, one of our waist gunners commandeered a Jeep, which we used for travel between missions. We headed for the town of Angeles for some food. We had a few drinks before we started. Mac was driving. We noticed a bunch of piglets on the road. Mac said, "Let's have a barbecue." We stopped the Jeep and circled the piglets. As we got them encircled, they started squirming and squeaking very loudly. At that time we heard a shot gun blast. The Filipino farmer was protecting his piglets. We all took off by jumping on the Jeep and made dust.

During other visits near Clark Field, we noticed a lot of Japanese planes left all over the field, damage of course by the Japanese before they left.

One visit was near the field where a high mountain contained caves in which Japanese had stored ammunition. The caves were loaded with equipment. The Japanese had left in a hurry. The towns near Clark Field had Japanese airplane equipment stored in shacks and garages, so when we bombed the field, they could not be damaged but were hidden from view. Near the middle of the mountain we visited was a fresh water pond. The water was cool and refreshing.

During our stay at Clark Field, Philippines, we were issued one case of beer every month. In order to cool beer, since refrigerators were not available, we used to take the beer in our barracks bags and tie the bags in the bomb bay of the plane. Then when we reached altitude, we cranked the bomb bay doors open, tied the bags to the structure of the catwalk, and thus cooled the beer. Usually this happened during plane testing of fuel consumption and practice.

One of the most frightening things and that I feared most during our long mission flights over water was plane malfunctions and being forced to ditch in the vast Pacific Ocean, shark-infested, with no good chance of survival. The B-24 was not as sturdy as a B-17 Flying Fortress. B-17s were known to fly back with huge holes in the wings. A B-24 would sink like a rock. Although we practiced ditching in large pools, with our inflatable rafts, we knew in an actual ditch by a B-24, chances were not good for survival.

Incident

During our stay at Clark Field in the Philippines, we occasionally had to perform guard duty on our planes. The Japanese were still in the surrounding hills, and at night they came down to the plane area and blew several tails off the planes, making them useless.

During one evening another crew member and I were guarding our plane. We had carbines to use if we noticed any action. While my companion and I were sitting on our Jeep, we heard a noise several feet away. As we looked, something dropped from a tree as we both opened fire. To our amazement it was a monkey that got away, not a Japanese.

During another escapade on our confiscated Jeep, four of us ventured out toward a town ten miles away. We arrived in a village at dusk and stumbled into a bamboo hut area. On approaching a unit, Mac the driver parked the Jeep with the bumper against a corner support of the hut. Since the huts did not have any glass on the windows but just an opening, we all stood up on the Jeep and looked in. To our surprise we saw a GI on the floor on top of a Filipino girl having sex. The noise interrupted the GI and he looked

B-24 crew. Standing, left to right: Michael Badolato, Francis Smith, Robert Arnold, Robert Baze, Steve Dubicz, and the author. Kneeling, left to right: Leroy Olsak, Ankle Molver, and Charles Alumbaugh.

The author in front of B-24 at West Palm Beach Airport when the only B-24 left still flying visited Florida in 1996.

Only B-24 still flying today, in 1996.

The author at discharge in November 1945, Newark, New Jersey.

China bombing.

Army of the United States

SEPARATION QUALIFICATION RECORD
SAVE THIS FORM — IT WILL NOT BE REPLACED IF LOST

This record of job assignments and special training received in the Army is furnished to the soldier when he leaves the service. In its preparation, information is taken from available Army records and supplemented by personal interview. The information about civilian education and work experience is based on the individual's own statements. The veteran may present this document to former employers, prospective employers, representatives of schools or colleges, or use it in any other way that may prove beneficial to him.

1. LAST NAME—FIRST NAME—MIDDLE INITIAL				MILITARY OCCUPATIONAL ASSIGNMENTS		
NICHOLS, JOHN A.				10. MONTHS	11. GRADE	12. MILITARY OCCUPATIONAL SPECIALTY
2. ARMY SERIAL No.	3. GRADE	4. SOCIAL SECURITY No.		1	Pvt	Basic Training
11 093 251	S/Sgt			8	Pvt	Airplane and Engine Mechanic (747)
5. PERMANENT MAILING ADDRESS (Street, City, County, State)				13	S/Sgt	Flight Maintenance Gunner (748)
30 Popler Street Boston, Mass.						
6. DATE OF ENTRY INTO ACTIVE SERVICE	7. DATE OF SEPARATION	8. DATE OF BIRTH				
6 Mar 1943	28 Nov 1945	30 Dec 1922				
9. PLACE OF SEPARATION						
AAF Separation Base Port of Newark, Newark, N. J.						

SUMMARY OF MILITARY OCCUPATIONS

13. TITLE—DESCRIPTION—RELATED CIVILIAN OCCUPATION

AIRPLANE AND ENGINE MECHANIC: Performed prescribed inspections and maintenance of aircraft. Examined portions of aircraft such as wings, fuselage, stabilizers, propeller, and landing gear for evidence of damage or wear. Corrected such defects by appropriate maintenance, minor repairs, adjustments or unit replacement. Manipulated controls in cockpit to insure proper operation and alignment of flight control system. Dismounted and replaced aircraft engines using mechanic's tools and equipment and technical orders as a guide to maintenance procedures.

FLIGHT MAINTENANCE GUNNER: Assisted pilot in the operation of multi-engined airplane B-24 by maintaining a constant check on its mechanical functioning. Noted readings of engine and navigation instruments, reported any indication of malfunctioning and maintained a log of engine performance. Made limited repairs and mechanical adjustments while in flight. Assisted pilot in deciding whether airplane should be grounded when serious malfunctioning developed. Reported needed repairs to maintenance crews. Fired 50 caliber guns in combat.

WD AGO FORM 100
1 JUL 1945

This form supersedes WD AGO Form 100, 15 July 1944, which will not be used.

MILITARY EDUCATION

14. NAME OR TYPE OF SCHOOL—COURSE OR CURRICULUM—DURATION—DESCRIPTION

Aviation Cadet School, Preflight and Primary training, 5 months completed 47 hrs flying time including 25 hrs solo flying time, 1943.

Airplane and Engine Mechanics School, completed 24 weeks course in Airplane and Engine Mechanic, 1944.

Aerial Gunnery School, Completed 6 weeks course in Aerial Gunnery, 1944.

CIVILIAN EDUCATION

15. HIGHEST GRADE COMPLETED	16. DEGREES OR DIPLOMAS	17. YEAR LEFT SCHOOL	OTHER TRAINING OR SCHOOLING	
12	Diploma	1942	20. COURSE—NAME AND ADDRESS OF SCHOOL—DATE	21. DURATION
18. NAME AND ADDRESS OF LAST SCHOOL ATTENDED			Mechanical Drawing Course Mass. School of Trade, Boston, Mass.	6 months
Boston English High School Boston, Mass.				
19. MAJOR COURSES OF STUDY				
Commercial				

CIVILIAN OCCUPATIONS

22. TITLE—NAME AND ADDRESS OF EMPLOYER—INCLUSIVE DATES—DESCRIPTION

RECEIVING AND SHIPPING CHECKER: Lawson & Hubbard Co., Boston, Mass. 1942 to 1943; Received and shipped merchandise. Handled petty cash vouchers. Possesses knowledge of Railroad and mail rates. Performed typewriting, controlled records including incoming and outgoing vouchers.

ADDITIONAL INFORMATION

23. REMARKS

24. SIGNATURE OF PERSON BEING SEPARATED	25. SIGNATURE OF SEPARATION CLASSIFICATION OFFICER	26. NAME OF OFFICER (Typed or Stamped)
John A. Nichols	*Francis M. Schuck*	FRANCIS M. SCHUCK Capt. AC

AIR MEDAL AND RIBBONS

GUNNERS WINGS

ARMY AIR FORCES
Certificate of Appreciation
FOR WAR SERVICE

TO

JOHN A. NICHOLS

I CANNOT meet you personally to thank you for a job well done; nor can I hope to put in written words the great hope I have for your success in future life.

Together we built the striking force that swept the Luftwaffe from the skies and broke the German power to resist. The total might of that striking force was then unleashed upon the Japanese. Although you no longer play an active military part, the contribution you made to the Air Forces was essential in making us the greatest team in the world.

The ties that bound us under stress of combat must not be broken in peacetime. Together we share the responsibility for guarding our country in the air. We who stay will never forget the part you have played while in uniform. We know you will continue to play a comparable role as a civilian. As our ways part, let me wish you God speed and the best of luck on your road in life. Our gratitude and respect go with you.

COMMANDING GENERAL
ARMY AIR FORCES

Some planes.

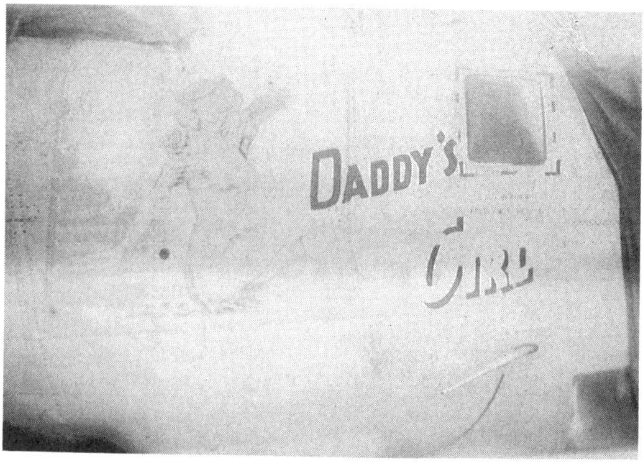
DADDY'S
GIRL

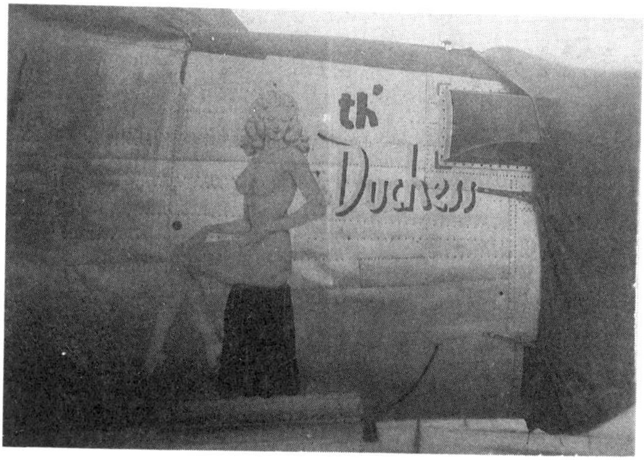
th'
Duchess

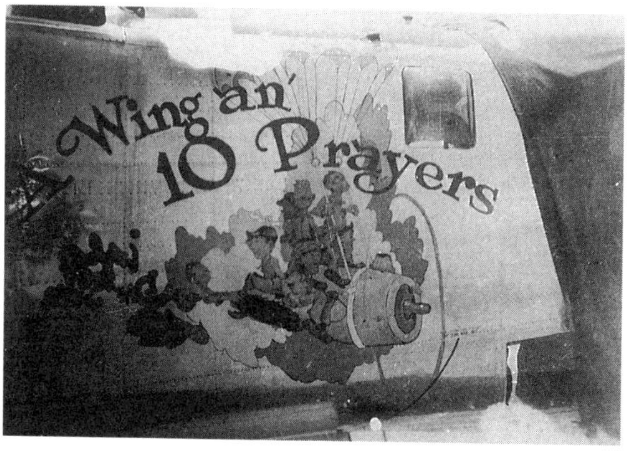
Wing an'
10 Prayers

JOHN A. NICHOLS

To you who answered the call of your country and served in its Armed Forces to bring about the total defeat of the enemy, I extend the heartfelt thanks of a grateful Nation. As one of the Nation's finest, you undertook the most severe task one can be called upon to perform. Because you demonstrated the fortitude, resourcefulness and calm judgment necessary to carry out that task, we now look to you for leadership and example in further exalting our country in peace.

Harry Truman

THE WHITE HOUSE

PILOT FLIGHT RECORD
AND LOG BOOK
TYPE 5D-3

BREAKDOWN OF TRIP TIME INTO CLASSIFICATIONS						REMARKS
INSTRUMENT	INSTRUCTION	DAY	NIGHT	DUAL	SOLO	INSTRUCTOR SHOULD ENTER IN THIS COLUMN THE NATURE OF EACH MANEUVER IN WHICH INSTRUCTION IS GIVEN, AND THE TIME SPENT THEREON, AND SHALL ATTEST EACH SUCH ENTRY WITH HIS INITIALS, PILOT CERTIFICATE NUMBER, AND PERTINENT RATING.
				22 30	10 39	
				0 45		
					02 28	All previous practiced
				00 36		maneuvers
					02 34	daily.
				00 42		
					02 31	
				01 31		Pylon Eights
					04 06	Loops & Snap Rolls
				00 35		
					01 25	
				26 39	20 43	ENTER IN THIS COLUMN DETAILS OF ANY SERIOUS DAMAGE TO AIRCRAFT. IF MORE SPACE THAN THAT PROVIDED ABOVE IS NEEDED FOR ANY DETAILS OF FLIGHT INSTRUCTION OR AIRCRAFT DAMAGE, USE PAGES PROVIDED IN BACK OF BOOK.
CARRY TOTALS FORWARD TO TOP OF NEXT PAGE						

United States Army

Army Air Forces Technical Training Command

Pvt. John A. Nichols, 11093251

is awarded this

Certificate

for satisfactory completion of a course in

Fundamentals of Teaching
for
Instructors of Airplane Mechanics

February 29 , 1943   _____ Lt. Col., A.C.
                                        Director of Training

Seymour Johnson Field, North Carolina

Borneo bombing.

Catwalk in bomb bay of B-24.

Bombs in bomb bay.

Clark Field, Philippines.

Air cadet.

up. Our eyes met and he started to swear at us and reached for his .45 near him. Mac immediately dropped down and started to pull away straight ahead. This resulted with the corner pole being pushed away, which caused the hut to collapse, and the yelling and swearing by the girl and the GI inside drowned our ears as the bamboo shack came down. After that we headed for our tent area.

During our stay at Clark Field, Philippines, we used B-24 aircraft with various names painted on the sides of the nose area. These names were of sexy girls, such as the Duchess, Slightly Dangerous, Kansas City Kitty, Round Trip Ticket, Daddy's Girl, Missing You, etc.

When a visiting general came to inspect our squadron, he insisted we repaint the girls and put clothes on them. Our squadron artist, who claimed he worked for Walt Disney, painted on clear cellophane clothes! In other words he put clothes on the girls (clear cellophane).

Plane Names

Some of the planes in our squadron were named (painted on the side of the fuselage).

Sleepy Time Gal
The Duchess
On a Wing and 10 Prayers
Kansas City Kitty
Missin' You
Slightly Dangerous
Daddy's Girl
Round Trip Ticket
Cocktail Hour
Queen Ann
Bread and Wine in 49

Tent Living

During our stay in New Guinea, Clark Field, Philippines, Okinawa, and other islands, our basic quarters were tents. There were six bunks to a tent. Usually the tent flaps were rolled up in a U-shape to catch any rainwater to be used for shaving and washing clothes. It was not a very comfortable living. The squadron had a shower area, which we used by wrapping a towel around us as we walked to the showers. In the Philippines we had Filipino girls do our laundry, so we had to wrap towels around us to be proper while the girls walked around the squadron area.

Our drinking water was in certain stations with plastic containers, spiked with atabrene (yellow in color) to protect from malaria. After drinking this water for a few weeks, we took on a yellow complexion. The water tasted awful, full of chlorine.

The mess halls were centrally located and were constructed of wood with corrugated metal roofs. Army food was not the best. It consisted of Spam, Spam, and more Spam. Plus powdered eggs, powdered milk, etc.

We had our .45-caliber guns with us under our bunks while we slept, in case attacked by Japanese, especially while at Clark Field, Philippines. There were Japanese soldiers in the surrounding area even after the Philippines were captured. During our long missions, the mess hall prepared lunches to eat while flying. One time we had fried chicken. The legs were very long and I swear they were sea gulls!

Also during our stay in Clark Field, a few squadron members decided to make their own liquor by gathering all the C-ration dried fruit such as raisins, fermenting them, and extracting the liquor, which was called "White Lightning." They even tried rice wine. Needless to say this was very powerful. One or two who had too much to drink actually had their hair turn completely white and had other physical ailments.

Diary Excerpts

MAY 7, 1945

We heard the good news about Germany surrendering. We hoped it would bring an end to the Pacific War. Since Germany was defeated we felt it will be a matter of time before Japan would be next.

MAY 14, 1945

Flew test hop; weather was very bad. Test flights were necessary to make sure planes were in good order.

Fifth Mission

MAY 22, 1945

Took off at 06:15 today for a mission over Toshien, Formosa. We had four (4) 2000-pound bombs. The target was very cloudy, so we dropped bombs on a secondary target. No flak or interception. Formosa now is called Taiwan.

This was the first mission to Formosa. The two-thousand-pound bombs packed a lot of punch. They would devastate a target if hit directly.

When the bombs hit, we could see huge explosions and smoke.

Most of these cities changed their names when the Chinese Nationalists took over Formosa.

Sixth Mission

MAY 26, 1945

We took off for a mission over Kiirun, Formosa at 8:00 A.M. We hit the target at 12:15. This time we saw flak. The bursts look like black powder, no noise, almost harmless, but potentially very,

very dangerous. One burst was close and we got hit by getting approximately ten holes in the plane. You never hear the anti-aircraft bursts. They are silent and almost beautiful as they puff out, almost like Fourth of July fireworks. From a plane you do not hear the explosion, and of course the puffs are black, not colored.

This was the first time we received flak. The bursts were very close in order for us to get flak holes. If one of these fragments had hit a vital part of the plane, such as a fuel line, propeller, or engine, it would have been very serious. The hits sounded like rocks hitting the aluminum skin of the plane. If these pieces hit the plexiglass domes of our turrets, they would cause serious harm to the gunners. Every turret had twin .50-caliber machine guns.

Seventh Mission

MAY 31, 1945

This mission was over Taihoki, Formosa. We took off at 7:15 A.M., and hit target at 12:30. This time the flak was very intense. The squadron ahead of us lost a plane to flak. Our plane got a flak hole. We got a point credit towards our total earnings, which determines returning home. The more holes or hits, the more extra points.

When the plane ahead of us was hit, it banked sharply to the left and went into a spin. We did not notice anyone parachuting out. We ourselves banked sharply and got away as quickly as possible. When we returned to base, all were saddened by the loss of the first plane. It was a severe blow to our morale.

Eighth Mission

JUNE 2, 1945

We took off for Kiirun, Formosa, at 7:10 after we had to

change our plane due to a small problem. We took off in a hurry and caught up with our squadron. We hit the target and saw only four bursts of flak, no hits on our plane. Our squadron had waited for us to catch up, since when flying over a target, we flew a formation, in order to protect ourselves from Zeros. If we were a single plane, the fighter had the advantage.

Ninth Mission

JUNE 5, 1945

We took off for Formosa, very bad weather. We could not find the target but dropped bombs on land, no particular target. Although we had radar, when severe clouds were covering our target, we generally did not drop the bombs indiscriminately, because of civilian casualties. However, on this mission we dropped the bombs because of very serious weather. Also, when flying into clouds, we scattered in different directions and altitudes to avoid accidentally hitting other planes.

Tenth Mission

JUNE 13, 1945

Mission over Takao, Formosa. This time we carried homemade fire bombs. The bombs were fifty-gallon drums filled with gasoline and jelly substance. At the end of each drum, there were two (2) hand grenades wired to go off on impact. On the way to the target, I noticed one drum leaking in the bomb bay catwalk. I got a waist gunner to use some old clothing to wipe out the jelly, since this would be very dangerous. Because of the higher altitude we were flying, the jelly expanded and started to leak out of the drums. We were extremely worried since a spark would set off the homemade bombs, made from napalm. As the bombs hit, you could see large fires spreading on a very wide area. The napalm bombs were usually for trying to destroy the target by fire, since on impact the napalm would spread over a wide area, constantly burning a path. It was very hard for ground crews to put out the fire. We carried twelve drums on one drop mission.

Eleventh Mission

JUNE 19, 1945

Mission over Kiirun, Formosa. We took off at 6:20 A.M. carrying eight (8) thousand-pound bombs. Over target we had light flak. One burst came very close at eleven o'clock. After our bombs fell, we saw big fires and smoke, which could be seen far away. Two planes got flak holes but not our plane. We landed at approximately 15:15. The Mission took approximately 8 hours and 55 minutes. Compared to the European theater, our missions were twice as long and sometimes, three or four times as long.

Each time we flew over a target and the first run was not exactly on the right path for the best bomb run, we tried again. However, each time the ground flak was getting closer and closer. I was hoping that on each mission we did not make more than one run over the target.

JUNE 24, 1945

We left Clark Field and flew to Palawan Island carrying paratroopers for practice run, in preparation of an attack on Japan. Our bomb bays were converted into plywood seats for the paratroopers. The troopers would be equipped with gear and some with small powered scooters. The troopers were completely laden with equipment, parachutes, helmets, rifles, machine guns, extra ammunition, etc. I really felt so sorry for them, for they were so young and with no fear of their ordeal. I thought how many of them would be killed even before they reached the ground. The plan for this invasion must have been so vast and detailed as to use thousands and thousands of troopers.

Twelfth Mission

JUNE 26, 1945

We took off at 6:30 for a mission over Borneo from Palawan Island. We hit a target in Borneo, mainly an airstrip. No flak or interception. We landed at 18:10. total flying time 11:40 hours. (See picture of this strike.) We hit this airstrip in order to prevent Japan from harassing our rear position as the U.S. jumped and skipped Japanese installations in order to neutralize their effort.

Thirteenth Mission

JUNE 28, 1945

Another mission over southern Borneo. We took off at 6:30. Our formation was ahead of our plane, so we made a single plane run over target. Again we bombed an airstrip. The squadron was almost intercepted by three (3) Zeros, but they did not come close. There were eight .50-caliber machine guns on every plane, times 6 planes means 48 guns trained on the Zero, so they had a healthy respect not to come close. We landed at 19:45, flight time 13 hours and 15 minutes. These are very long missions, over water, which is very tiring and dangerous, compared with short missions in the European theater of war. Our worry was more about water flying than interceptions or flak.

The Japanese had spread out all over the South Pacific before the U.S. forces started their counterattack. They (Japanese) had built airstrips all over. In order for U.S. to make sure rear guard action would not take place, we bombed rear bases repeatedly.

JUNE 30, 1945

We came back to Clark Field from Palawan Island, Philippines. It was very hard to get settled on a regular home base. Flying from Clark Field one day and receiving orders to fly to another base made it very tiring and unsettling. However, this was war and no questions were asked.

Fourteenth Mission

JULY 6, 1945

The mission over Heiti, Formosa, took off at 6:15 carrying (240) twenty-pound bombs. This time we made three runs over target. This was very dangerous since flak guns got closer every run. However, flak was very light. We landed at 16:15, flight time approximately ten (10) hours. We received a flak hole, but it was not approved. More points means you a get back to the States sooner. This is ironical since a good flak burst can knock the plane down, which means forget going home.

We actually were not looking forward to receive flak holes, knowing that a direct hit would be the end, but why not take credit if it happened?

Fifteenth Mission

JULY 11, 1945

Fifteenth mission, over Shinchiku, Formosa. We took off at 6:40 and hit the target about 11:30. After our bombs hit, great billows of smoke could be seen for miles around. A very large fire was observed. One plane was hit by flak, no damage. We received an extra point for a flak hole. We landed at 15:30. Time of flight: 8:50 hours.

These missions seem to be routine now. I guess we could be

considered veterans. However one can be still aware of the danger we were in. Since a veteran crew can get to be naive and make mistakes, I was always concerned and was very aware of all steps towards checking for every precaution and safety.

I repeatedly checked engine performance, fuel consumption, hydraulic and electrical systems. If changes occurred it was best to be alert so corrective measures could be taken. I always thought the worst would happen.

10
Okinawa

We took off at 6:30 for Ie-Shima, a small island off the coast of Okinawa. We landed at 12:45. We left Clark Field in moving preliminarily to Okinawa, in order to set an advanced base. Ie-Shima is in the northeast corner of Okinawa.

11
Mission over Shanghai, China

Sixteenth Mission

JULY 24, 1945

Sixteenth mission, over Shanghai. We took off at 6:00 A.M. Flying over Shanghai at this time, it was the biggest air strike of the Pacific war. I believe there were over four hundred planes. We passed over our target three times and each time flak was getting closer and closer. Finally we heard flak hitting our plane like sand particles. Our plane got eleven holes. I saw one plane get a direct hit and it went down in flames.

After bombs away the bombardier said he saw blood in the area. We were concerned someone was hit. However, this was the hydraulic fluid pouring all over, which made walking dangerous. I called for one waist gunner to help me contain the leaks. We took spare overflow tubing lines and couplings from the hydraulic fluid reservoir tank and coupled the severed lines. This took us a long time, but it finally contained the leaks. We worked frantically for about two hours. We filled more fluid from reserve tanks to make up the lost fluid. These severed lines went to the bomb bay door operators, the plane brakes, and the flaps.

The area around the bombardier to the right of the aircraft was a complete mess, with the hydraulic fluid sprayed all over the floor, sides, and ceiling. It was dangerous to walk since one could slip on the fluid. At first it was confusing as to what to do and what actually was damaged. When we got our thoughts together, we immediately acted to do something to restore the hydraulic system.

We radioed the air base in Okinawa regarding our problem and asked base to be alert re our arrival in case we encountered further unknown damage to the plane. Before we finally arrived over Ie-Shima airstrip, we checked the landing gear in flight which, appeared okay, not flat.

When we landed, the plane began to swerve like a crazy yo-yo, but luckily we came to a stop in the middle of the runway. Apparently the flak had pierced both landing tires.

Excess red hydraulic fluid was leaking from the plane onto the airstrip, so the fire engines and ambulances were rushed to the side of the plane. They thought someone was wounded or killed for all that fluid, which they thought was blood, to be leaking from the plane. Fortunately, everyone was fine.

Later I found a piece of shrapnel about three inches long by half an inch wide imbedded under my upper turret seat. The seat had a half-inch armor plate, but the underside was lined with half-inch plywood and the shrapnel (which I still have as a souvenir today) imbedded in the plywood. If there had been no armor plate, I would not be here today since you can imagine where it would have landed.

During this episode, while flying, you did not have time to think clearly. However, after our flight in the briefing room, we suddenly felt the critical irony of it. Quite an experience. I commend the help I got from our crew to come through all this dangerous event. During the flight we also lost our No. 1 engine super charger in the flak burst.

We landed at approximately 1:30 (flight time 7:50).

Undoubtedly this was the most dangerous mission I had ever experienced. However, I also was very grateful we came out of it alive. It felt good to know that we inflicted a severe attack on the enemy. If the flak hits had damaged an engine or a vital part of the plane it would have been all over for our crew.

During a mission over Formosa while flying formation in a twelve (12) plane flight, a tragedy occurred just before we hit the target. A nose gunner on a plane to our right, whom I noticed while the nose gunner was trying to clear his .50-caliber machine gun, reached under the gun cradle for a check on the entering belt of .50-caliber ammunition. His elbow struck the handle switch and the cradle came down on his body, crushing him to death. I saw this and felt helpless to do anything. We finally broke radio silence and informed the pilot of his plane of this tragedy.

JULY 25, 1945
We flew back to Clark Field, Philippines.

AUGUST 9, 1945
We visited the city of Manila today. The city is much bigger than I thought. I never saw so much ruin, other than at Nagasaki and Tokyo. All the main buildings are in ruins. The Japanese really damaged the city before they left.

The women of Spanish and Filipino ancestry are strikingly beautiful. The Filipino people were so friendly to all of us. They would offer rice cookies and are very helpful in offering us to do laundry. They were grateful that we had liberated them from Japan. You can see their relief in their happy faces.

AUGUST 12, 1945
We flew to a field south of Manila today to pick up paratroopers and fly to Okinawa. The plane bomb bays were equipped with plywood seats to carry troopers over Japan for an invasion. As soon as we loaded the plane, we got orders to unload. A plane from our squadron had crashed due to a short air strip and unbalanced loading. All passengers and crew were lost in a fire when the plane crashed. We returned to Clark Field, empty. When we took off, we could see the remnants of the plane that crashed, lying below us.

AUGUST 13, 1945

We flew a load of paratroopers from Clark Field to Okinawa. We spent the night there. During the night at approximately 9:00, Japanese Kamikaze planes raided the naval ships in the harbor. We could hear the blasts as the suicide Zeros headed for their targets. This was a scary night.

From then on, while at Okinawa, we experienced terrible nights while we were sleeping in our squadron tents. The Japanese Kamikaze raids on the naval ships anchored in the bay continued all the time, sirens wailing all night long on several occasions. There was not too much damage, but every now and then, a suicide pilot had a near miss.

It is difficult to understand the lack of respect for a human being's life for these a suicide pilots. However, they were considered heroes back in Japan.

During one morning while sleeping in our squadron tent, we were awakened by a plane noise, which sounded very odd. The whining noise made us go outside. Our tent was at the bottom level of the runway of Yontan airstrip. As we looked up, we saw a C-47 stall and go down a few feet from us. We ran to the wreckage, but all aboard died by the crash and fire.

Apparently the plane took off with the wooden clamps still locking the ailerons. Plane crews locked them while the plane was on the ground to protect them from wind damaging the ailerons.

The crew aboard did not have the clamps removed. I can still see the pilot's eyes full of horror before he crashed. He realized what was wrong. When we arrived at the plane crash, we could see the charred bodies of the pilot and copilot in their seats.

Incident

While on Ie-Shima Island, Okinawa, during a few days between missions, several of us decided to make a raft out of a P-38 plane wing tanks. We split the tanks in two and joined them together with wood. Then we took canvas from a damaged tent and designed a sail.

The beach was beautiful and relaxing. Then four of us decided to take the raft out for a sail. We had extra wood strips as paddles. As soon as we got on, a swift current took us so fast that we jumped over and swam to shore while the raft disappeared rapidly out on the open ocean.

AUGUST 14, 1945

We returned to Clark Field from Okinawa. We were shuttling between Okinawa and Clark Field, Philippines, in order to establish a forward base in Okinawa. All our equipment had to be transported to Okinawa.

AUGUST 15, 1945

Today we received news that Japan had accepted terms of surrender. At last the war is over. We were overjoyed! The best news we have received for a long time.

Could this be the end of the war? It was hard to comprehend the reality. Is it possible that Japan was finally defeated? I was so happy that it was hard to believe. That evening we celebrated by opening a bottle of liquor we had saved. The crew was so happy that we celebrated all night.

AUGUST 22, 1945

The squadron moved to Okinawa. We were shown our area. We stayed for two nights. Now we did not mind the lazy waiting. The war was over. The tension was gone. No more live bombs in the plane.

AUGUST 23, 1945

We visited the surrounding area and saw Japanese burial sights on caves in the hill sides. We took pictures and enjoyed the surrounding area. That morning while six of us were resting in our tent, suddenly a figure entered. We thought it was a bear. It turned out to be an Okinawan dressed in a furry cape who wanted work.

AUGUST 24, 1945
We flew back to Clark Field to get our luggage and personal things so that we could establish Okinawa as our permanent base.

AUGUST 28, 1945
We flew back to Okinawa. There are rumors we are going to Japan.

The United States now was faced with a massive problem of how the forces were going to be dispersed. Not only the men but equipment. After the war there was a story that all the planes were to be stored in a field in Texas. One man made an offer to buy all the planes; perhaps it was thought to sell the equipment for scrap. However the man made a fortune by selling the high-octane gasoline in the tanks of the planes!

12
Weather and Reconnaissance over Tokyo and Nagasaki Bomb Site

SEPTEMBER 1, 1945
We were alerted by rumor to prepare for going to Japan. Rumors were flying around every day.

SEPTEMBER 10, 1945
We were again alerted but not to go to Japan, rather to break up the squadron and move to the States. I was hoping these rumors were true.

Seventeenth Mission

SEPTEMBER 14, 1945
A select crew of men were picked to fly over Japan for a reconnaissance and weather mission. Two flight engineers, two radio men, two navigators, etc. Our mission was to go over Tokyo—Osaka—Nagasaki—Kyushi.

We took off from Matsubi, Okinawa, at 5:30. We arrived over Tokyo at 10:45 and flew over the American fleet in Tokyo Bay. As described before the sight we saw was unbelievable.

Returning to Okinawa we were extremely worried about our fuel. Each plane had a different level of gas sight gauges. To be extremely cautious, I warned that we should conserve fuel. However we made it back to Okinawa safely. We landed at 18:45. The total flight was thirteen hours and fifteen minutes. We were extremely tired when we reached our bunks, still thinking of the terrible sight over Nagasaki.

SEPTEMBER 18, 1945
The first six planes left today for Yontan, Okinawa, first leg on going home. We are awaiting our turn.

SEPTEMBER 20, 1945
We left base on plane no. 255 for Yontan. We may have to stay here to transport prisoners of war to Manila. Hope it isn't too long.

SEPTEMBER 24, 1945
We lost our plane today. Another crew took it away. Rumors say we may go by boat, air transport command, or fly with another crew.

SEPTEMBER 28, 1945
We visited a yellow beach in Naha Bay. We had a ride on a "duck" boat to a transport ship. The Navy really lived very well. They had all fresh food and the best of everything. We "confiscated" some food for our crew. We traded two bottles of whiskey that we picked up in Clark Field for the food. We had fresh oranges for the first time in months.

OCTOBER 2, 1945
We took off at 3:15 for Clark Field, Philippines, and landed at 8:15. We picked up passengers and took off for Yontan.

OCTOBER 10, 1945
This day a big typhoon hit Okinawa. It was devastating. All the tents blew away. The mess halls were fabricated of corrugated

galvanized sheets and they blew away. Sheets would fly like wild birds. It was very dangerous. Several men were sliced by these sheets. I spent the night in an open 50-gallon drum, with my head and shoulders inside the drum and my legs outside. It was the only way to protect myself from flying objects. The rain woke me up all night. It was the most miserable night of my life.

The typhoon lingered all night and day. It was difficult to find food. Thank God for the K-rations. For a week we had nothing but canned Spam. We had it every way you can imagine. Plain Spam, powdered egg Spam, fried Spam, chopped Spam, etc. Can you imagine eating this all week?

OCTOBER 11, 1945

We were assigned to the Hundredth crew to leave for the States. We can not wait for the day.

OCTOBER 12, 1945

We rebuilt a small shack from salvaged wood. We began to live again inside a dry enclosure.

OCTOBER 25, 1945

We were still waiting our turn to leave for the States. The waiting is terrible. Some tragic news today. One crew member, a nose gunner from another squadron crew, was found dead behind a tree. His girl friend had found another boy she was going to marry. He blew his brains out with his .45 pistol. The strain of war is very real. It gets to you very quickly, especially when you receive bad news from home.

OCTOBER 27, 1945

We were processed today to leave for the States during the next few days. They mentioned to me that I would head for Fort Devens in Massachusetts, for the separation center. We were told we would fly from Okinawa to Clark Field and then home.

NOVEMBER 8, 1945
    We left Okinawa for Clark Field. We took a C-46 from Naha to Clark Air Field.

13
Flight Home

NOVEMBER 9, 1945
We were processed for shipment to the States and assigned a B-24M. I felt, this is it at last.

NOVEMBER 10, 1945
We flew a test hop to determining fuel consumption. Every plane had its own fuel characteristics on sight gauges, etc.

NOVEMBER 11, 1945
Awaiting to leave. Since we already had our plane assignment, I was not concerned.

NOVEMBER 12, 1945
We took off at 5:30 for Guam. The trip took ten hours and ten minutes. We had trouble with No. 4 engine manifold and stayed in Guam one extra day to install a new waste gate motor.

NOVEMBER 14, 1945
We took off at 6:30 from Guam, landing at Kwajalein at 16.25. We stayed overnight, then took off the next morning for Honolulu.

NOVEMBER 15 & 16, 1945
We took off from Honolulu at 16:30 and landed in Mather Field, California, at 6:50. Total flying time: fourteen hours and

twenty minutes. We did not mind the long flight since we were going home. We were actually singing and in good spirits.

NOVEMBER 16, 1945

We landed in Mather Field in the United States of America. I cannot describe the feeling of returning to America. It suddenly struck me that all was over and I was safely home. After the danger of flying over vast areas of water, with young airmen with no fear of enemy or dangers of water, you cannot imagine how great it was to finally find yourself out of danger. No more missions, no more preparing for flights, no more being shot at. What a wonderful feeling, looking forward to heading for home. The ordeal is finally over.

All this terrible experience was now over. I almost kissed the ground as I left the plane. The crew was hugging each other with joy.

I did not fully realize how dangerous it was during these missions: avoiding flak, from Japanese Zeros and really the most dangerous, flying over the vast Pacific Ocean. I could not wait to send a telegram to my family to let them know I had returned safely.

14
Separation

I was notified that I would be headed for Newark, New Jersey, soon to be separated. I left by train for final separation. After a three-day train trip East, I arrived in New Jersey and was finally discharged.

I reenlisted in the reserved for three more years. Today at seventy-four years, I'm living in Canton, Massachusetts, where I am semi-retired. I have three children and five grandchildren.

The GI Bill helped me go to college, continuing my engineering. I started a company selling industrial dryers and industrial air systems.

I still feel I'm living on borrowed time, thanking God that I came home safely and have a good life.

I often think of the crew and events we shared together, hoping that all are safe and with their families, for we all did our part to make this world safe from any ambitious men who thought they could take over the world. Many crises will occur in this strange world, but America must be aware and diligent in helping to preserve the democracies and oppressed people. It is very satisfying to know that in a very small way I did my part to achieve a victory for the United States of America.

Appendix
Important Sites

Taiwan

Formally called Formosa. Now a separate nation (Chinese). Chang Kai-shek moved his people from Mainland China to this island when the Chinese Communists took China over in 1949.

This Island is approximately 235 miles long by 90 miles wide. The Japanese took this island from China when they invaded during World War II.

The capital now is Taipei. Many of the target cities shown on missions now have different names. The island is approximately 90 miles off the Chinese coast. The island is mountainous. The Chinese call the island, Taiwan, meaning terraced bay. Portuguese sailors in 1590 named it Formosa, meaning beautiful island. The Nationalist government on Formosa also controls several islands in the Taiwan Straits, which separates Taiwan and China. These islands include the Quemoy, Matsu, and Pescadores groups.

Okinawa

Located northeast of Taiwan (formerly Formosa) approximately a thousand miles from Tokyo. Youtan Air Field was located on a plateau. This island was a target of the Japanese Kamikaze suicide plane attacks, especially the naval ships anchored in the bay.

Okinawa is the largest and most important island of the Ryukus group, a chain of islands in the north Pacific Ocean. Okinawa covers 554 square miles and has over one million people.

Okinawa was under the Japanese before and during most of World War II, 1939–1945. The United States captured the island during the war and administered the island until 1972.

One of the bloodiest battles of World War II was fought on Okinawa.

The United States forces landed on April 1, 1945, and the battle lasted until June 1945.

Ie-Shima

A small island north off Okinawa with an airstrip, where we landed several times.

Tarawa

One of the bloodiest battles of World War II in the South Pacific Theatre was fought here, a small island in a large chain.

On November 30, 1943, the United States Marines attacked Tarawa with the amphibious LVT's. However, when the flat-bottomed Higgins went in, they were caught on reefs with only three feet of water. This meant that the Marines had to wade in hundreds of yards under severe fire. They were almost eliminated by the Japanese.

The Japanese had 4,500 men on the island. The United States lost 991 Marines dead and 2,341 wounded. The Japanese lost all, except for 17 who came out alive.

The United States learned a lot from the experience of this landing.

Palawan Island, Philippines

This was a beautiful island just southwest of Manila. The beaches were like paradise, with palm trees all over the area.
I said that if I got back after the war, I would definitely visit this island. I never did.

Rabaul

Part of the New Britain Islands. This Japanese stronghold was spared an invasion. However, it was pounded by bombers, which sank supply ships. About a hundred thousand Japanese defended the island but were spared by United States' isolating the island and not invading.

The Philippines

MacArthur decided to invade the island of Leyte in the central Philippines in the fall of 1944. It was the largest force ever to be used in an invasion.

This was the first time Japan used the Kamikaze (suicide pilots). The Leyte fighting continued until the end of 1944. On January 9, 1945, United States forces landed in the island of Luzon and fought toward Manila, which was captured in March of 1945. The Japanese withdrew into the mountains. Clark Field is in Luzon.

About 350,000 Japanese soldiers were killed in the Philippines and approximately 14,000 United States soldiers died.

The capture of the Philippines was a crushing blow to Japan.

Places as Targets

WEWAK   Location: New Guinea, where Japanese had a stronghold
RABAUL   Near New Guinea, New Britain Island where Japanese had a compound and air strip
FORMOSA   Island to which I flew several missions. (now Taiwan)
SHANGHAI   Site of one large mission in which a 400-plane raid occurred. On this raid in China, flak cut our hydraulic lines.
BORNEO   Several of my missions flew here to bomb Japanese airstrips.

```
Total Missions Combat            = 16
Recon. and Weather and Misc.     = 21
                                   37
```

Stations during Terms of Service

Reported to North Station, Boston, Massachusetts
Fort Devens, Massachusetts
Nashville, Tennessee
Montgomery, Alabama. Maxwell Air Field
Douglas, Georgia. Primary Flight School
Greensboro, North Carolina
Goldsboro, North Carolina
Fort Myers, Florida
Douglas Aircraft, Santa Monica, California
Mather Airfield, California
Riverside, California (March Field)
Hamilton Air Base, San Francisco, California
Hawaii

Canton Island
Admiralty Islands
Biak, New Guinea
Nadzab Base, New Guinea
Clark Field, Philippines
Ie-Shima, Okinawa
Youtan, Okinawa

Index

Alomogordo, 2
Angeles, 26
Atomic bomb, 3
A-20, 11
Author's note, *xiii*

B-17, 10
B-24, *x*, 31
Biak Island, 16
Borneo, 42, 53

C-47, 24
Canton Island, 15
China, 25
Clark Field, 25
Contents, *vii*
Crew, 29

Decorations, *xi*, 36
Dedication, *v*
Douglas Aircraft, *xi*, 11
Douglas, Georgia, 7

English High, 4

First Mission, 22
Formosa, 51
Fort Myers, 10

Guam, 67

Hamilton Air Base, 13
Hawaii, 15
Heiti, 54
Hiroshima, 3

Ie-Shima, 56, 58, 60, 72
Introduction, *xi*

Kamakazi, 60
Kiirun, 49

Lae, 16
Lengayan Gulf, 25
Leyte, 25

Manila, 59
Mather, 13
Maxwell, 5

Nadzab, 18
Nagasaki, 1
Naha, 66
New Britain Island, 23, 73
New Guinea, 16

Okinawa, 56, 71

Palau, 25
Palawan Island, 73
Philippines, 73
Preface, *ix*

Pre-flight, 7
Primary, 9
PT-17, 7

Rabaul, 23, 73
Riverside Air Base, 12

Shanghai, 25, 57
Shinchiku, 54

Taihoki, 50

Taiwan, 71
Tarawa, 15, 72
Tokyo, 63
Toshien, 49
Truman, 40

Wewak, 22

Yangtse, 26
Yontan, 60